THE ART OF WORKING WITH IDIOTS

UPGRADED BOOKS

CONTENTS

ALSO BY UPGRADED BOOKS

INTRODUCTION

The workplace is a living ecosystem – part ambition, part dysfunction, and part mystery meat from the break room fridge. Inside it, a particular breed thrives: the obliviously confident, the terminally self-important, and the blissfully unaware. They are both the cause of and the reason for your daily mental headache. This book is not here to make them better. It's here to make *you* better at surviving them, benefiting from their chaos, and maybe even enjoying the absurd theater of it all.

This book is your workplace coping tool. Sure, it's full of jokes, sarcasm, and a healthy dose of eye-rolling, but tucked between the laughs are fundamental, practical strategies to keep your sanity intact.

You'll find advice that can apply to everyone in the workforce - from the new intern that's figuring out the lay of the land to the "I'm over it" manager who's one email away from moving to a cabin in the woods.

I'm not here to judge (unless judging is part of your coping mechanism - then okay, it's totally valid).

I'm here to give you permission to laugh at the absurdity, feel validated in your frustration, and maybe - just maybe - learn a trick or two to navigate the office jungle with style.

This book contains 100 ways for "artfully" working with less-than-brilliant colleagues. These tips are grouped into themes so you can flip to any section for a dose of humor and help.

Disclaimer: *Some of these ideas are meant to be laughed at, not lived out. If a tip sounds like it could land you in HR's office, court, or the evening news, maybe just enjoy it in theory.*

So dive in, smirk often, and remember: you're not alone.

We're all in the same circus... some of us just have better seats.

Happy reading,

Sam

THE OFFICE WILDLIFE SPECIES GUIDE

E*very office is its own wilderness.*

This is your guide for spotting the local wildlife.

Once you learn their patterns, their strange calls, and their natural habitats, you'll see the office for what it really is: a fascinating collection of personalities, blunders, and cautionary tales.

You might recognize some of them immediately if you've had the pleasure of working with them.

The Control Freak in a Manager's Badge

They call it "attention to detail." We call it "standing over your shoulder, breathing down your neck while you adjust the font size." Their motto? "If you want something done right, micromanage until everyone quits."

Warning: Extended exposure may cause spontaneous eye rolls and recurring stress dreams.

The Accidental Boss

Promoted not because of talent, but because the universe has a sick sense of humor. They've mastered the art of nodding sagely while secretly Googling or ChatGPTing the terms their team just used.

Warning: Do not assume leadership actually knows what's going on. Ever.

The Vanishing Act

Officially employed, spiritually elsewhere. They've turned "looking busy" into performance art.

Warning: Side effects include sudden workloads that mysteriously become your problem.

Professor All-Knowing

The oracle who interrupts, over-explains, and "actually..."'s their way through every meeting.

Warning: Listening too long may cause permanent damage to your will to contribute.

The Human Newsfeed

They collect gossip like it's currency, then spend it recklessly.

Warning: Never confide – even "just this once." By lunch, it's company-wide knowledge.

The Drama Distributor

Every hiccup is a full-blown tragedy, starring them.

Warning: Approach cautiously. It may pull you into a storyline you never auditioned for.

The Boss's Shadow (a.k.a. Serial Suck-Up)

They laugh too hard, volunteer too fast, and mysteriously vanish when real work starts.

Warning: Keep your distance. Praise is their oxygen, and they're always short of breath.

The Playground Bully in Business Casual

Still running the same tactics from grade school, just with a dress code.

Warning: Confrontation fuels them. Starve them of reaction whenever possible.

The Snake in the Breakroom

Charming to your face, dagger-ready behind your back.

Warning: If they're smiling, double-check your calendar invites.

The Credit Collector

Your hard work, their standing ovation.

Warning: Document everything. Even your lunch break might end up in their highlight reel.

The Walking HR Violation

"It's just a joke," they say – every time HR winces.

Warning: Keep a safe paper trail. You'll need it.

The Human Podcast

One-sided conversations that make time slow to a crawl.

Warning: Escape routes should be planned in advance.

The Volume Problem

If decibels were productivity, they'd be CEO.

Warning: Earplugs recommended. Sanity not guaranteed.

PART I

ACKNOWLEDGING THE IDIOTS AMONG US

EMBRACE THE REALITY – IDIOTS EXIST EVERYWHERE

F irst step: acceptance. Every workplace has its token fools, and yours isn't a rare exception – it's a thriving ecosystem. Skip the shock; just nod to yourself like you've seen this movie before, and think, "Ah, yes, here we go – the idiots have arrived on cue."

YOU'RE NOT ALONE (MISERY LOVES COMPANY)

Your department's got them, accounting's got them, the rival firm across town has them, too. *Everyone* has horror stories about clueless coworkers or bosses. The next time you're trapped in meeting purgatory, just remind yourself: somewhere else, another poor soul is staring into the middle distance while their coworker explains email – again.

IDIOTS GONNA IDIOT – DON'T TRY TO CHANGE THE UNCHANGEABLE (AT LEAST, IMMEDIATELY)

Trying to fix an idiot is like trying to teach a pigeon calculus. You might make noise, they might flap, but nothing meaningful happens. Manage your expectations; you are not the appointed Idiot Whisperer.

4

DIAGNOSE THE "IDIOT" ISSUE – IGNORANCE, LAZINESS, OR TRUE INCOMPETENCE?

Not all idiocy is created equal. Before you sharpen your sarcasm, figure out what flavor of fool you're working with. Is your coworker uninformed (they simply don't know what they don't know), lazy (fully capable but unmotivated), or genuinely incompetent at their job? Each requires its own approach: educate, motivate, or quietly sidestep.

LOWER YOUR EXPECTATIONS
(WELCOME TO THE LOW BAR CLUB)

This is a self-preservation tactic, not cynicism: set the bar so low that any idiots can step over it without tripping! Then, when a miracle happens and they actually get it right, you can feel genuine – if slightly suspicious – joy! In short, don't expect genius from a proven idiot, and you won't face daily heartbreak.

6

USE HUMOR AS A SHIELD

Some errors are so absurd they deserve to be framed. Instead of rage-quitting, try to find the humor in it – smirk and mentally note it for your personal highlight reel. Yes, the CEO really did accidentally reply all with "WTF is this?". We will always have that memory.

KEEP PERSPECTIVE – IT'S (USUALLY) NOT LIFE OR DEATH

R emind yourself: *"This is just work."* Most office disasters won't end civilization, though some will test your will to live. That messed-up report or endless meeting won't matter in five years (heck, five days). If it's not going to make headlines or trigger an evacuation, breathe. It's just another page in the never-ending sitcom script that is your workplace.

8

KNOW YOUR TRIGGERS (AND PREPARE ACCORDINGLY)

I dentify exactly what drives you *crazy* about your resident office idiot. Is it Karen's know-it-all tone? Dave's constant procrastination? Pinpoint what pushes your buttons, then put up guardrails. Think of it as allergy prep: a mental antihistamine before the pollen storm of BS rolls in.

FIND A TINY SILVER LINING

As hard as it may be, try to spot one *redeeming* quality in the person who tests your patience. Maybe that utterly clueless colleague is at least **really** friendly, or the boss who can't use Excel always remembers birthdays. It might feel like searching for a needle in a haystack, but hang onto that shred of goodwill – it's a small emotional life raft in a sea of irritation.

DON'T JOIN THE IDIOT CLUB – STAY SELF-AWARE

A tongue-in-cheek warning: Idiocy spreads faster than office gossip. Maintain self-awareness so that *you* don't start adopting their bad habits out of frustration or apathy. For example, just because Tom forgets every deadline, don't let that make you slack on yours.

PART II

THE IDIOT ECONOMY

THE LAW OF IDIOT SUPPLY (THE ONLY UNLIMITED RESOURCE)

I diots multiply faster than office chairs in a start-up. With every new hiring round, it's likely that at least one is a fresh fool added to the ecosystem. Don't waste time dreaming of idiot-free days; accept that they're the most reliable thing your workplace will ever produce. Plan accordingly, like stocking up for storm season.

IDIOT INFLATION (WHEN EVERYTHING LOSES VALUE)

A s the idiot count rises, meetings, memos, and even time itself get cheaper – because they're wasted on nonsense. Suddenly, a one-hour meeting accomplishes the same as a two-sentence email, and morale tanks. Protect your sanity by treating your competence like gold in a failing currency: guard it, display it when necessary, but don't let it get squandered.

SUBSIDIZING STUPIDITY. SOMETIMES KNOWN AS "MANAGEMENT'S FAVORITE HOBBY."

The workplace often props up fools with praise, promotions, or "team player" awards. It's basically corporate welfare for incompetence. Instead of fuming, quietly stop volunteering as their safety net – let their bad ideas fall flat without your free overtime. Self-preservation beats unpaid sponsorship.

THE SCARCITY MYTH (SPOILER: IT'S A LIE)

Dreaming of an idiot-free office is like dreaming of meetings that end early. Fun to imagine, but not in this reality. Lower the fantasy bar: idiots aren't rare, they're renewable. Competence, sadly, is the endangered species here.

THE TRICKLE-DOWN FOOL EFFECT

I diocy at the top spreads like a company-wide virus. When a clueless executive sets the tone, entire departments adopt "good enough" as the new gospel. Your best defense? Translate the nonsense into real tasks, then quietly hold yourself to higher standards – even if it makes you look like an overachiever.

16

IDIOT BUBBLES (HYPE MACHINES
ON TWO LEGS)

E very office has that one overhyped fool treated like a genius. Everyone nods at their "vision" until the bubble bursts and disaster strikes. Don't hitch your credibility to their bandwagon – keep receipts, maintain distance, and enjoy the view when gravity finally does its job.

THE OPPORTUNITY COST OF IDIOCY (TIME YOU'LL NEVER GET BACK)

Every hour fixing someone's blunder is an hour you don't spend on your own priorities – or your life. That's the hidden idiot tax, and it compounds daily. Before you dive in, ask: Is this worth paying, or should I let the natural consequences do the teaching?

THE COMPETENCE BLACK MARKET

T his is where the real work gets done. When fools dominate the official channels, the competent few create underground alliances. Work gets traded quietly, projects move in secret, and sanity is preserved in hushed tones. Find your fellow competence smugglers – it's the only way deadlines survive.

THE LAW OF DIMINISHING RETURNS

S top debating fools. The longer you argue with an idiot, the less you get back. Eventually, you're not solving anything – you're auditioning for their clown show. Know when to cut your losses: smile, nod, and let reality handle the closing argument.

IDIOT BAILOUTS (GUESS WHO PICKS UP THE TAB?)

W hen fools fail, leadership often swoops in – not to remove them, but to protect them. Usually, by handing their workload to you. Master the art of polite redirection: "That sounds like something Bob should take the lead on." It's corporate judo, and it saves your back.

Closing Thought: *The Idiot Economy runs on over-supply, under-demand, and endless bailouts. Once you understand the rules, you stop being the sucker footing the bill. Treat your time like a premium stock, invest wisely in competent alliances, and never forget: in this market, competence is the rarest – and most valuable – asset.*

PART III

SPEAKING "IDIOTESE"

KEEP IT SIMPLE, SOLDIER (THINK KINDERGARTEN, NOT GRAD SCHOOL.)

With some coworkers, complexity is your enemy. Use short sentences, plain words, and visuals if you must. You're not writing a dissertation – you're building Ikea furniture with no manual. Make the instructions so clear that *even they* can't invent a new way to screw it up.

TRUST. BUT VERIFY

A nod from them does not equal comprehension – it often just means they want the conversation over. Ask them to repeat the plan back, or follow up with a short recap email. That way, when they inevitably forget, you've got receipts. Idiot-proofing means documenting reality.

PATIENCE IS A SURVIVAL TOOL. (CHANNEL YOUR INNER KINDERGARTEN TEACHER)

Sometimes you'll explain things twice. Sometimes ten times. Resist the urge to throw your laptop out the window, and instead rephrase, simplify, or break it into steps. It's less painful to repeat yourself now than to mop up the flaming wreckage of their "interpretation" later.

DRAW THEM A PICTURE

Words fail? Try diagrams, sketches, or flowcharts – even stick figures if necessary. Nothing drives home the point like a crude doodle of how their plan collapses. Bonus: visuals stick in memory, which means fewer excuses when they try the "oh, I forgot" routine.

SAVE THE SNARK (TEMPORARILY)

S arcasm may feel therapeutic, but chances are they'll miss it or misinterpret it. *"Sure, wing it, what could possibly go wrong?"* might be taken as genuine encouragement. Keep your wit holstered during actual instructions; unleash it later with a trusted coworker who deserves the performance.

CHOOSE YOUR HILLS TO DIE ON

N ot every misuse of jargon or bungled sentence needs correcting. If you fight every battle, you'll burn out before lunch. Save your energy for the misunderstandings that actually impact work; let the smaller slip-ups drift away like bad background noise.

BUILD A THIN BRIDGE

Sometimes, finding even the slightest shared interest makes communication easier. A joke about the local team, a quick comment on their dog obsession – anything to humanize the exchange. The goal isn't friendship; it's lubrication for smoother interactions when work conversations inevitably stall.

LEAD THEM TO THE WATER

Telling them they're wrong rarely works – leading questions, however, sometimes do. Ask how they think their idea would work in practice, or what they expect the client's reaction might be. Occasionally, they connect the dots themselves (miracles do happen). If not, at least you've mapped their brand of confusion.

29

PLAY PARROT (WITH PURPOSE)

R epeat their idea back in your own words, just to check alignment. Hearing "So, you want to delete the two customer databases without a backup?" might spark their long-lost survival instincts. At worst, you get clarity on just how bad their plan really is. At best, you save the day by catching the disaster early.

CONTROL YOUR FACE

Tone and body language betray you faster than words. If you're rolling your eyes, sighing, or dripping sarcasm into your delivery, they'll feel attacked and shut down. Practice your poker face and neutral voice – even if internally you're screaming. Keeping the idiot calm means the message has a fighting chance of landing.

Closing Thought: Communication with fools is less about brilliance and more about strategy. Keep it simple, keep it documented, and keep your face under control. In the end, surviving "Idiotese" is like surviving any foreign language immersion: smile, nod, repeat, and pray for subtitles.

PART IV

MEETINGS AND EMAILS

ALWAYS BRING AN AGENDA (YOUR SHIELD AGAINST CHAOS)

Without an agenda are basically improv theater, *and not the funny kind.* Send a roadmap ahead of time, and you'll have a built-in excuse to steer the group back when someone launches into a monologue about their dog's birthday party. Agendas are the traffic cones of office life – they won't stop the crash entirely, but they'll at least slow it down.

USE THE PARKING LOT

W hen someone derails the discussion with "what ifs" or off-topic rants, park it. "Great point, let's put that in the parking lot" sounds polite, but it's really code for "thanks, we're never coming back to that." Ninety percent of parked items vanish into oblivion, which is exactly where they belong.

33

SHARE THE FLOOR

Every office has a Loud Larry who treats meetings like open-mic night. The trick is to interrupt with grace: "Let's hear Linda's thoughts on this." Suddenly, you've both shut down Larry and pulled in someone who might actually add value. It's a one-two punch of diplomacy and survival.

GIVE THE DISRUPTOR A JOB

I f you know who's going to derail the meeting, assign them a role – note-taker, timekeeper, anything that keeps their mouth busy. "You're so detail-oriented, could you track the key points?" Translation: Please stop talking. It won't always work, but at least you tried to weaponize their energy.

THE "TECHNICAL DIFFICULTY" CARD

Virtual meetings offer one blessed loophole: fake connection issues. If someone is rambling beyond reason, "Oops, you froze – moving on" buys you peace. It's sneaky, but sometimes survival requires creative bandwidth management. Just don't overuse it, or they'll catch on eventually.

END WITH A RECAP (LOCK THE DOOR BEHIND THEM)

Before everyone bolts, take two minutes to spell out who's doing what. "So Bob owns X, Alice handles Y..." Not only does this reduce confusion, it blocks the classic escape hatch: "I didn't know I was supposed to do that." Recaps are your idiot insurance policy.

EMAILS MUST BE SHORT

The attention span of some coworkers hovers between goldfish and fruit fly. Put the key point right at the top, bold if needed, and keep the rest in bullets. If they only read the subject line, they should still know what you want. *Think telegram, not novel.*

STRATEGIC CCS

Accountability skyrockets when someone's boss is looped in. "Per our conversation, John (CC'd) and I are expecting your update by Friday" suddenly makes deadlines real. Use sparingly – overdo it and you'll look like HR's tattletale cousin. But when stakes are high, nothing sharpens focus like the boss's watchful eye.

STOP THE REPLY-ALLPOCALYPSE

One careless "Reply All" from the office fool can nuke the inboxes of fifty innocent bystanders. Preach email etiquette early: keep replies targeted. If needed, use BCC as your silent bodyguard. A little coaching today saves the company from a week of "Thanks!" spam tomorrow.

GUARD YOUR OFF-HOURS

S ome fools love firing off midnight "urgent" emails that are about as urgent as reorganizing the break-room mug cabinet. Resist the Pavlovian ping. Train them by replying only during work hours, or set up a delayed send. Eventually, even the densest will figure out you're not on-call for their imaginary emergencies.

Closing Thought: *Meetings and emails are where idiots thrive if unchecked. Keep them structured, short, and idiot-proof, and you'll spend less time cleaning up chaos — and more time pretending to work while scrolling memes.*

PART V

IDIOT-PROOFING YOUR WORK

PAD YOUR TIMELINES WITH AN "IDIOT BUFFER."

Deadlines are a fragile concept in Idiot Land. If you need something by Friday, tell them Wednesday. It's the same principle as setting your clock ten minutes fast – except this time the "clock" is a colleague who thinks "end of day Tuesday" means "I'll look at it sometime next week." A built-in cushion keeps you calm, even when they inevitably stumble in late with excuses. Consider it your project's airbags.

FOLLOW UP, FOLLOW UP,
FOLLOW UP

Think of reminders as oxygen – idiots can't function without them. One request is never enough. You'll need nudges, check-ins, and the occasional calendar ping to keep the hamster wheel spinning. Rotate your approach – email today, quick chat tomorrow, calendar invite the next – like a one-person accountability orchestra. It feels like babysitting, because it is. But it's still better than the alternative: a failed deliverable and a long speech from your boss about "ownership."

DOCUMENT EVERYTHING (BECAUSE MEMORY IS OPTIONAL)

I f it's not written down, it didn't happen. Keep notes, summaries, and receipts of every assignment: "Just to recap, you'll handle A while I handle B." This way, when someone inevitably develops selective amnesia, you have proof. Documentation also doubles as a reminder for them AND a shield for you when the blame games start. HR and managers love receipts. *Give them receipts.*

ALWAYS HAVE A PLAN B (AND PROBABLY C)

Trusting the office flake with a mission-critical task is like letting a toddler carry the wedding cake. Hope they succeed, but have alternatives in place. Draft a backup outline, line up an alternate teammate, or quietly prep a workaround. It's a little extra effort up front, but infinitely less stressful than explaining to leadership why the whole project imploded because you gave "Crash Gordon" the keys to the car.

SIMPLIFY TASKS FOR MAXIMUM SURVIVAL

Never hand an idiot a vague assignment like "own the client presentation." That's how you end up with 37 slides of irrelevant clip art. Break it down into painfully clear, step-by-step instructions: "Add data to slides 1–5, email them to me by Thursday." The less wiggle room for creative interpretation, the safer your sanity.

VERIFY THE WORK (TRUST, BUT
VERIFY – THE SEQUEL)

J ust because they say "all done" doesn't mean it's actually done – or even legible. Always spot-check before passing their work along to anyone important. Catching a glaring typo or missing attachment in private is infinitely better than explaining it in a meeting. It feels unfair to recheck someone else's job, but think of it as quality control for your own reputation.

PLAY TO WHATEVER STRENGTHS
THEY HAVE (YES, EVEN TINY ONES)

Nobody is completely useless – they can at least serve as a bad example. But honestly, most people have *something*. The math-phobic chatterbox might still be a decent client charmer; the chronically late guy might be creative when he actually shows up. Identify that one sliver of competence and point them toward it. They'll feel valued, and you'll keep the heavy lifting with people you actually trust.

MINIMIZE DEPENDENCY ON THE WORST OFFENDERS

D on't let the weakest link be the sole guardian of the chain. Spread responsibilities or pair them with someone competent so the project doesn't grind to a halt when they inevitably "forget." Structure workflows like redundancies on an airplane: if one engine flames out, you don't crash immediately. Protect yourself from single points of idiocy.

SAY NO TO BECOMING THE PERMANENT CRUTCH

E very office has a repeat offender who expects you to bail them out. And every time you say yes, you reinforce it. The next time they dump their work on your desk, politely push back: "I've got my own deadlines – have you tried using [tool/guide/etc.]?" Helping occasionally is teamwork; being their unpaid assistant is exploitation. Draw the line now, or you'll be their safety net forever.

PROTECT YOUR CREDIT (SHINE IN YOUR OWN SPOTLIGHT)

I n the land of glory-hogs, your contributions can vanish faster than free snacks in the break room. Don't let it happen. Share progress updates with your boss and team in a way that clearly outlines what you've delivered: "Report draft complete, waiting on John's figures." That way, your role is visible, and the office klepto has fewer opportunities to "accidentally" claim your ideas.

Closing Thought: Idiot-proofing isn't pessimism, it's project survival. Build buffers, document everything, and don't be afraid to say no. Think of it as workplace judo: use their weaknesses to protect your own strength.

PART VI

ZEN AND THE ART OF
IDIOT MANAGEMENT

FIND A VENT BUDDY (YOUR EMOTIONAL FIRST AID KIT)

Pick one person you trust to hear your idiot horror stories – preferably someone who won't repeat them at happy hour. A five-minute rant to a friend who says, "Yep, that's insane," will do wonders to release some steam. It's cheaper than therapy and safer than yelling directly at the idiot. Extra credit: rotate your vent buddies occasionally so nobody burns out from listening to your catalog of idiocy.

KEEP A HUMOR STASH

Stockpile memes, clips, or inside jokes that instantly reset your mood. A quick scroll through workplace humor can take you from "I'll commit arson" to "Okay, that was dumb, but at least laughably dumb." Laughter doesn't erase the idiot, but it does lower your blood pressure enough to face them again. For maximum impact, save one or two gems just for "nuclear" moments – those days when the idiocy peaks so high you can practically hear circus music.

MOVE YOUR BODY (PREFERABLY AWAY FROM THEM)

W hen your patience meter flashes red, get up. Walk, stretch, do jumping jacks in the stairwell – whatever burns off irritation before it eats you alive. Bonus: idiots rarely follow you on these breaks because that would require effort. Even two minutes of motion can flip your brain from fight-or-flight to "Okay, I can get through this."

BREATHE (YES, REALLY)

S ounds basic, but deep breaths actually calm your nervous system before you say something career-limiting. Inhale, exhale, remind yourself, "I will not let this idiot take me down." You don't become enlightened, but you do look impressively composed. And the beauty is, no one can call you out for breathing – it's the one coping mechanism that works anywhere, anytime, without raising suspicion.

DON'T TAKE IT PERSONALLY
(NATURE DOCUMENTARY MODE)

Their nonsense is about them, not you. Pretend you're narrating a wildlife special: "Here, we see the office idiot forwarding a chain email as though it were urgent news." Observation over indignation keeps you detached – and entertained. It helps to remind yourself they probably act like this everywhere, which means it's not personal malice – it's just their natural state of being.

CREATE IDIOT-FREE ZONES

Schedule breaks that are completely fool-free. Lunch with a sane colleague, a solo walk, or fifteen quiet minutes with music all count. Think of it as rinsing the stupidity off your brain before diving back in. The trick is to guard these spaces fiercely – if someone tries to drag the chaos in, politely decline and reclaim your bubble.

TURN IT INTO A GAME

Make a secret bingo card of predictable behaviors: "interrupts," "forgets attachment," "asks irrelevant questions." Instead of rage, you rack up points. Winning feels better than fuming – and yes, you're allowed to reward yourself with something stronger than a gold star. Just keep the game to yourself; idiots don't take kindly to finding out they're your personal sport.

JOURNAL THE ABSURDITY

Write it all down – the facepalm quotes, the jaw-dropping mistakes, the sheer audacity. Ranting on paper gets it out of your system, and months later, it reads like comedy. Who knows? You might accidentally draft the next great office satire. If nothing else, journaling ensures that when someone tries to gaslight you – "That never happened" – you've got the written record of every absurd episode.

REWARD YOURSELF FOR SURVIVAL

E ach time you survive a meeting without snapping, pay yourself in treats – snacks, Netflix binges, small indulgences. If dogs get biscuits for not barking, you deserve at least a cookie for not flipping a desk. Training works both ways. Over time, you'll actually start associating idiot encounters with something positive: "Yes, that meeting was awful, but now I get sushi."

MAINTAIN A LIFE BEYOND IDIOTVILLE

The best defense is perspective. If your evenings are full of hobbies, family, and things you actually enjoy, Dullard Dan's blunders shrink in importance. Work becomes just one slice of your life pie – not the whole stale thing. The more vibrant the rest of your world is, the less oxygen the office idiocy has to consume you. This is your insurance policy against burnout.

Closing Thought: Managing idiots is more about not letting them take you down with them rather than becoming a saint. You can vent, laugh, breathe, or even turn it into a game, but the key is remembering that your sanity matters more than their nonsense. Stay grounded, reward yourself for surviving, and keep a life outside their orbit. Idiots may always exist, but they don't get to own your peace of mind unless you hand them the keys!

PART VII

THRIVING IN SPITE OF IDIOCY

SHINE IN THE CHAOS (JUST DON'T
BE A SPOTLIGHT HOG)

When everyone around you is fumbling the basics, doing your job well suddenly looks like an Olympic-level genius. Deliver quality work consistently, and you'll stand out – no need for fireworks. But keep the smug switch off; nothing kills goodwill faster than looking like you're performing a TED Talk while everyone else is still trying to open PowerPoint. Quiet competence always beats loud arrogance.

VOLUNTEER FOR THE RIGHT PROJECTS (BEFORE THEY HAND IT TO CAPTAIN TRAINWRECK)

I f you see a critical assignment dangling in the wrong hands, grab it. Co-lead, rescue, or step in strategically before the damage spreads. Just be selective: don't volunteer for every dumpster fire project. Choose projects that match your strengths, where your success is both visible and undeniable. Nothing builds your rep faster than stepping in when others panic and walking away with a win.

TREAT IDIOT ENCOUNTERS LIKE UNPAID TRAINING

Yes, it's infuriating. But each time you survive someone's incompetence, you're sharpening your own toolkit. The guy who loses every file? He's teaching you the fine art of documentation. The boss who mumbles jargon like it's a second language? You're becoming a translator. It may not be glamorous, but when you later deal with a competent colleague, you'll feel like you've been playing on "hard mode" all along – and suddenly everything is easy mode.

COLLECT MENTORS AND ALLIES (YOUR EXIT STRATEGY AND YOUR INSURANCE)

D on't waste your career surrounded only by the clueless. Hunt down the competent ones – whether they're across the hall, in another department, or someone you meet at a conference. Mentors give perspective, allies give support, and together they remind you you're not the only functioning adult in the building. They'll also be the ones opening doors when it's time to move up or move out.

65

BUILD YOUR REPUTATION (BECAUSE BRAND MATTERS)

I f the office feels like noise, you want to be the signal. Keep your higher-ups updated on your wins. Share credit generously but make sure your own role or contributions don't disappear. Aim to be known for two things: results and calm. "They always deliver, even when everything's falling apart" is the reputation that gets remembered when promotions are being handed out – or when leadership is desperate for someone who won't embarrass them.

SPEAK UP

Sometimes the incompetence isn't just annoying – it's damaging. That's when you document examples, line up evidence, and present it constructively. "These reports keep going out with errors, here's the impact, here's a fix" lands way better than "John is terrible." Always bring a solution to the table so you're seen as the problem-solver, not the complainer. Management notices the difference.

67

USE HUMOR AS SOCIAL GLUE

The team is scrambling to fix yet another blunder. Morale is tanking. This is your moment. A sharp, inclusive joke or witty observation can reset the mood and keep people moving. Think "Well, now we know what not to put in the client presentation" rather than roasting the idiot directly. You're not auditioning for stand-up, but the ability to keep people laughing while rowing uphill is leadership gold.

CONSIDER A TRANSFER
(SOMETIMES SURVIVAL MEANS
CHANGING FLOORS)

I f you're stuck in Idiot Headquarters, scope out other departments. Not every corner of the company is a lost cause. Volunteer on cross-team projects, network quietly, and look for openings where competence is actually valued. A lateral move can feel like stepping from quicksand onto solid ground – even if there's still the occasional puddle.

NETWORK OUTSIDE THE BUILDING (PROOF THAT NORMAL PEOPLE EXIST)

Stay connected with former coworkers, attend industry events, and keep your LinkedIn alive. It serves two purposes: (1) it reminds you that functional professionals really do exist, and (2) it gives you lifelines when it's time to bail. Plus, sharing war stories with outsiders often nets you new coping tactics – or at least the relief of someone else saying, "Yeah, my office is that dumb too."

KEEP LEVELING UP (WHILE THEY'RE STILL WRESTLING WITH THE PRINTER)

Don't let the incompetence drag you down into apathy. Use the irritation as motivation: sign up for courses, learn new software, build certifications, and grow your skill set. Every upgrade makes you more valuable – and more portable. While Bob is rebooting his computer for the third time today, you'll be preparing for your next promotion. Progress is the sharpest form of payback.

Closing Thought: Idiots don't have to anchor your career. If anything, they make your competence easier to spot. Build skills, build allies, and build a reputation for results. At some point, you'll outgrow the nonsense and move up – or move on. And when leadership looks around for who can handle real responsibility, they won't remember the guy swearing at the copier. They'll remember you.

PART VIII

MANAGING THE IDIOT

SET CRYSTAL-CLEAR EXPECTATIONS (PAINT-BY-NUMBERS STYLE)

The first defense against chaos is clarity. "Finish the report ASAP" is an engraved invitation for excuses. Spell it out: "Complete the Q3 sales report by Thursday at 5 PM with sections A, B, and C." Over-communication may feel silly, but vague instructions are where idiots thrive. Lay down the lane markers, or they'll claim the road didn't exist.

TRAINING BEFORE TERMINATING

Sometimes the "idiot" is just someone who never got proper training. Pair them with a mentor, send them to a workshop, or toss them an online course. If they improve, congratulations – you've upgraded them. If not, you've documented your attempt at redemption, which HR will love when you escalate. Either way, you win.

CATCH THEM DOING SOMETHING RIGHT

Yes, even a broken clock is correct twice a day. When your problem child actually delivers something decent, acknowledge it. "That summary was clear and on time – nice work." Small doses of positive reinforcement make it more likely they'll stumble into success again. Plus, it shows you're fair, not just waiting to pounce.

DELEGATE LIKE A CHESS PLAYER

Handing the big client pitch to your mumbling analyst? That's sabotage. Instead, align strengths to tasks: put the detail-obsessed on data, the smooth talker in front of clients, and the fumbler on something safely contained. Delegation is more than work distribution; it's also risk management. Your job is to keep the wrong pieces from toppling the board.

REGULAR CHECK-INS (PREVENTIVE MAINTENANCE)

D on't wait until the project is a smoldering crater. Schedule quick one-on-ones or mid-project reviews. Catch mistakes early, when they're just potholes instead of sinkholes. It's a bit like car oil changes – you can either do them regularly, or you can wait for the engine to seize on the highway. Your choice.

DOCUMENT, DOCUMENT, DOCUMENT

P erformance conversations without records are just arguments with louder voices. Keep dated notes, emails, and specifics: "Missed client deadline on April 12 after two reminders." Documentation protects you, gives HR ammunition, and makes the conversation less "You're incompetent" and more "Here are five receipts of the same failure." Harder to argue with evidence.

HAVE THE TOUGH CONVERSATIONS (SKIP THE TAP-DANCING)

N o one likes giving negative feedback, but avoiding it just prolongs the mess. Sit down privately, be specific ("On Project X, Y happened, causing Z issue"), and explain the impact. Then listen – maybe there's a real obstacle. Deliver expectations for next time, clearly and calmly. Empathy is fine, but sugarcoating incompetence is managerial malpractice.

HR ISN'T THE ENEMY (USE THE SYSTEM)

W hen progress flatlines, it might be time to call HR. They know the drill for Performance Improvement Plans (PIP), warnings, and (if it's necessary) exits. If you've documented and followed procedure, HR will be your shield. Skip them, and you're left twisting in the wind when things go legal.

PROTECT YOUR HIGH PERFORMERS

The danger of one idiot on the team is that your stars quietly pick up the slack – until they burn out and quit. Watch for this. Acknowledge when they cover for others, rebalance workloads, and make sure competence doesn't become a punishment. Losing good people because you ignored the idiot problem is the managerial equivalent of setting your house on fire to kill a fly.

BUILD A CULTURE OF LEARNING (NOT EXCUSES)

E ncourage the whole team to keep improving – lunch-and-learns, retrospectives, or just normalizing "I don't know" as an acceptable phrase. High performers thrive in environments that reward curiosity. The worst? They reveal themselves by resisting. Either way, you raise the floor and the ceiling at once. Growth culture makes it harder for fools to hide.

Closing Thought: Managing idiots is all about systems. Clarity, documentation, training, and accountability form the foundation that protects your team from collapse. Do it right, and you'll keep your high performers happy, your projects intact, and your sanity mostly preserved. Do it wrong, and you'll spend your days running an adult daycare.

PART IX

HR'S PLAYBOOK

LOOK FOR PATTERNS (THE IDIOT SMOKE DETECTOR)

H R sees across departments, which means you're the only ones who notice when five people quit in three months, all muttering about "Bob in Accounting." Don't ignore that smoke alarm. Track recurring complaints, turnover trends, and common grievances. Idiocy is rarely subtle – it leaves a trail. Early detection allows you to step in before the talent drain turns into a stampede. Imagine yourself as the epidemiologist of workplace nonsense: trace the outbreak, isolate the carrier, and apply treatment before the whole floor is infected.

IMPLEMENT PREVENTIVE TRAINING (RAISE THE FLOOR)

The simplest way to reduce workplace idiocy? Teach people the stuff they should have learned years ago. Offer sessions on communication basics, time management, and the software everyone pretends to understand but clearly doesn't. Make them group sessions so no one feels targeted. The best employees will sharpen their skills, the borderline ones might improve, and the stubborn idiots will at least lose the excuse of ignorance. "Remember that email etiquette workshop? Yes, that covered not replying ALL to the CEO."

ENCOURAGE A FEEDBACK CULTURE (ANONYMITY IS YOUR FRIEND)

I diocy thrives in silence. Employees usually spot issues long before HR does, but they keep quiet out of fear. Create safe channels: anonymous surveys, feedback forms, or quarterly town halls where people can vent without painting a target on themselves. Stress that feedback isn't tattling but a way to ensure quality control for the workplace. When patterns emerge, act. A single complaint may be noise; a chorus of them is very likely a red flag. Better to address it while it's still in the "annoying" stage than when it's a lawsuit.

USE MENTORSHIP OR BUDDY SYSTEMS (PAIRING THE WILD CARD)

Sometimes what a struggling employee needs isn't another HR memo but a patient guide. Set up mentorship programs where newer or weaker performers shadow competent ones. The rookie might actually flourish with guidance, and the oblivious jerk might finally pick up on social cues. Choose mentors wisely: assigning your top performer to babysit the department disaster is a morale hazard. But with the right matches, knowledge spreads, bad habits shrink, and the culture gets stronger. Sweeten the deal by recognizing mentors who do the heavy lifting.

85

REINFORCE POLICIES AND SET NON-NEGOTIABLES (BECAUSE "I DIDN'T KNOW" IS THEIR FAVORITE EXCUSE)

R e-state your policies when needed and make expectations crystal clear. "Professional Courtesy Reminder: Please respond to emails within 24 hours" may sound basic, but it sets the standard. HR should also back managers who enforce these rules so they're not left alone in the trenches. When someone inevitably protests, "Nobody told me," you'll have a nice policy handbook that says otherwise.

INTERVENE EARLY (BEFORE THE DUMPSTER FIRE)

The longer you ignore a brewing conflict, the messier it gets. When employees bring concerns, act quickly: mediate, clarify roles, or investigate if necessary. Don't wait until it escalates to passive-aggressive email chains or whispered gossip in the break room. Catch it early, and you might salvage both the relationship and the project. Waiting until it's a five-alarm fire just means HR spends more time cleaning up ashes than preventing them.

MASTER THE ART OF CORPORATE TRANSLATION (TURNING "JIM IS AN IDIOT" INTO POLICY LANGUAGE)

One of HR's underappreciated superpowers is translation. A manager may say, "My team hates working with Jim because he screws up everything," but your job is to turn that into: "There are concerns regarding Jim's performance and its impact on team morale." Documentation has to sound professional, not personal. You're essentially polishing turd into something HR-compliant – it still stinks, but now it's presentable for the file.

STAY IMPARTIAL AND CONFIDENTIAL (HR AS SWITZERLAND)

Yes, employees come to you desperate to hear validation like, "Wow, Bob really *is* the worst." Resist. Stay neutral. Gather facts, keep confidences, and manage with professionalism. If word gets out that HR gossips, your credibility implodes, and suddenly, nobody will bring issues forward. Whether you're dealing with the accuser or the accused, your job is to stay centered. Think mediator, not drinking buddy.

SUPPORT AND GUIDE THE MANAGERS (HALF OF THEM DON'T KNOW WHAT THEY'RE DOING EITHER)

Not every manager is skilled at handling underperformers. Some avoid conflict, others bulldoze through it. HR should coach them – offer scripts, best practices, even role-play tough conversations. Remind them of available tools like performance plans, probation, or structured coaching if available. Many managers tolerate bad employees for far too long simply because they don't know the process for fixing the problem. Give them the confidence they need to act decisively and fairly.

HIRE AND ONBOARD BETTER (CUT OFF THE SUPPLY LINE)

P revention beats firefighting. Bad hires cause years of headaches, so refine your recruitment. Screen harder: add skill tests, use behavioral interviews, and check references thoroughly. Look for red flags, like a candidate who blames "toxic workplaces" at every job they've ever had. Then, onboard properly – don't just toss new hires in the deep end. Train them, set expectations, and give them tools to succeed. Idiocy thrives when people start confused and stay confused. A little rigor up front saves everyone years of grief later.

Closing Thought: HR as the Last Line of Defense. When idiocy runs unchecked, it becomes expensive, toxic, and contagious. HR has the unique vantage point and authority to notice patterns, set expectations, and intervene before the damage spreads.. Spot the problems early, translate them into action, and filter the pipeline for better hires. Because in the end, preventing idiots is far easier than rehabilitating them.

PART X

THE IDIOT ENLIGHTENMENT

EMBRACE THE SERENITY (OR AT LEAST PRETEND TO)

That famous serenity prayer works beautifully at the office – just swap "things" for "people." Accept the idiots you can't change, find the courage to confront the ones you might redirect, and pray for the wisdom to know which is which. Not every mess is yours to clean up, and not every person is yours to fix. The sooner you stop treating hopeless coworkers as DIY projects, the lighter your day feels.

FOCUS ON YOUR GROWTH, NOT THEIR FAILURES

I t's easy to obsess over how Kevin still can't figure out the copier after three years, but obsessing won't advance your career. Use the downtime created by their incompetence to sharpen your own skills. Learn software, pick up certifications, polish leadership chops. You can't upgrade someone else's brain, but you can make yours more valuable. The bigger your personal growth, the less their failures sting – and the quicker you'll outpace them.

COLLECT THE COMEDY

One day, you'll retell these horror stories at happy hour, and people will gasp, "No way that actually happened." But it did – and it's material. Treat today's office disasters as tomorrow's stand-up routines. When Carol hits "Reply All" to the entire company again, picture yourself laughing about it later instead of getting annoyed now. Humor reframes the pain. Plus, it gives you stories that make you the most entertaining person at dinner parties.

ACKNOWLEDGE YOUR RESILIENCE
(PAT YOURSELF ON THE BACK)

L ook at you – still standing after years of daily idiocy. Every time you navigate a meeting full of nonsense and still deliver, you're leveling up in patience, diplomacy, and survival skills. Idiots are your involuntary personal trainers, forcing you to build thicker skin and a sharper wit. Sure, it's a miserable gym, but you're walking out stronger than most. Give yourself the credit: you've earned stripes in a field no MBA covers.

DON'T SINK TO THEIR LEVEL

The temptation is real – "If they don't care, why should I?" But professionalism is about you, not them. Keep showing up on time, being respectful, and doing the work with integrity. Treating even the worst offenders with baseline civility shows character. You're refusing to mud-wrestle with pigs. You'll stay clean, and they'll stay pigs.

SHARE THE SURVIVAL GUIDE

When a new hire's eyes widen in horror after their first week, be the voice of calm. Pull them aside and let them know that, "It's not just you. Here's how to cope." Mentor them in the dark art of idiot-handling – quiet patience, careful documentation, emergency humor. This way, you build an ally and it has the benefit of reinforcing your own mastery. You're passing the torch of wisdom, one shell-shocked recruit at a time.

APPRECIATE THE NON-IDIOTS (YES, THEY EXIST)

A mid the chaos, there are always a few competent, decent humans holding it together. Don't overlook them. Thank them. Work with them. Befriend them. The good ones are like Wi-Fi in a dead zone: precious and worth clinging to. Shift your focus toward them, and the noise of the fools will shrink. Work may never be perfect, but good colleagues make the job survivable – and sometimes even enjoyable.

RECOGNIZE WHEN IT'S BEYOND REPAIR

Some workplaces are so saturated with incompetence that it's not worth the therapy bills. If the idiots run the show, your health is shot, and growth is a pipe dream, it's time to move on. You've earned a black belt in Idiot Management and now you're ready for a better dojo. No shame in leaving. Sanity is worth more than a paycheck.

EXIT GRACEFULLY (SILENT VICTORY LAP)

As tempting as it is to send a mass "good luck surviving with these clowns" email, don't. Quit clean. Thank people for "the opportunities," shake hands, and walk out with dignity. Why? Because reputations matter and nothing screams power like leaving without bitterness. You win by moving on, not by lighting up the building behind you. Your last laugh is knowing you'll never again have to sit through that pointless Monday meeting.

GET THE LAST LAUGH

E very ridiculous incident, every brain-melting conversation – it's all raw material. Maybe you'll write a blog, maybe a book, maybe just be the funniest person at the dinner parties. Convert office absurdities into material that can entertain and educate.

That's the ultimate enlightenment: idiots may drain your time, but they'll fuel your creativity forever. Keep notes, keep it light, and keep moving forward. That's how you truly beat them.

THANK YOU FOR READING THIS BOOK!

I would be incredibly grateful if you could take just 30 seconds to leave me a review!

Reviews are crucial for an author's livelihood, yet they can be surprisingly hard to get.

The more reviews my books receive, the more I can continue pursuing my love for creating books.

If you have any thoughts about this book, please leave a review and let me know.

- Sam

Printed in Dunstable, United Kingdom

75593302R00077